Poems
FOR THE PASTOR

Poems
FOR THE PASTOR

The Reflections and Poetry of
RICHARD A. PHIPPS

RESOURCE *Publications* · Eugene, Oregon

POEMS FOR THE PASTOR

ISBN 13: 978-1-55635-727-5
www.wipfandstock.com

Manufactured in the U.S.A.

Dedicated to the memory of
my loving wife, Diane.
She heard "trumpets" the day
our Lord took her home!

CONTENTS

Dear Pastor,

This collection of poems is for you! Many times, we struggle for the words to express our deepest desires, hurts, expectations, counsel, and prayers for our beloved flock of sinners saved by grace. Many times that same struggle extends to us and our families.

I have found throughout my ministry those words can often best be expressed through verse. In no way are these poems a claim to poetic artistry, but simply an offering from my heart to yours.

My prayer is that you can apply these poems to your own ministry, and that possibly they can help strengthen your own faith and endurance as you run this difficult race of shepherding! Use them to His glory!

Richard A. Phipps

❧ THE CHURCH

DID YOUR church used to be great? Did they used to fill the pews every Sunday at one time, but now they are struggling just to get by?

This was the case at a church in Tennessee where I used to pastor. They once ran over six hundred in worship, but had dwindled to less than one hundred by the time I arrived. One day, I spoke with one of the previous pastors about the church in its hay day. He told me the church had once thrived because of particular members who lived life on *purpose* for God. This poem mentions some of those thriving members, and puts all he told me into perspective rhyme.

We Used to Have Passion

We used to have passion, the children ran strong,
the hallways were full, and classrooms were in song!
Pitter patter feet as they weaved through the crowd,
screaming and squirming with laughter so loud.
What was the secret? I think I can tell ya!
It was the God-given passion found in Ovelle!

We used to have passion, students flocked in review,
two hundred at least, in bright orange filled our pews!
Short ones, tall ones, thin ones and round,
no textbooks in hand, just God's Word could be found!
What was the secret? Come closer a little!
It was the God-given passion found in John Riddle!

Nurses and families, old ones and young,
all seem to come to praise Him in song!
What was the secret? Did the Pastor make the calls?
Was he somehow gifted to do it all?
He told me, *"No! My time was not rationed!*
I just sat back and watched the members with passion!"

HAVE YOU ever had members who tend to focus on *non-Kingdom* matters? I am speaking of the kind of focus that prohibits them from keeping their eyes on God's purpose and mission? Often, that focus is directed to things like the *sacred* church building! Then when maintenance problems occur within the building's glory, and budget needs are short, *fear* begins to set in. That *fear* is difficult to overcome, and we fight to keep our members faithful in God's ability to handle the *peripheral things*. The same God, the Creator of all things, in whom they have placed their trust for salvation, the same God who proved the greatest miracle of all when He defeated death, the unlimited "*Spring of Living Water*," for some reason now cannot be trusted to maintain a building!

The problem is even more compounded when the building is a one hundred twenty five-year masterpiece of construction and beauty! The church I described in the previous poem was such a place. It was magnificent! Surrounded by dark mahogany, a majestic horseshoe balcony, glorious chandeliers, a huge pipe organ, and stain-glass windows, I felt like Charles Spurgeon every time I stepped into the pulpit! The building was once full in its prime, but by the time I arrived, the numbers had dwindled to a faithful few who remembered the glory days, and struggled with maintaining the building they loved. That wasn't easy, when just turning on the sanctuary lights cost the church over $200 an hour!

Are you there, too?

A Building of Old

Clang, splash, drip, rumble!
These are the sounds of a building of old!
Hiss, boom, plop, crumble!
Never ending do problems seem to unfold!

Heat, air, lights, gas!
Much is e'er needed to satisfy all!
Paper, phones, salaries, alas!
Will they be paid with a budget so tall?

An old building erected for six hundred or more,
Such numbers could handle with ease!
But an active faithful, less five hundred from before,
Now struggles to ensure it does please!

What is the answer to the dilemma they face?
Hard choices must to them befall!
But forget not God is ne'er gone without trace!
His power and riches exceed all!

FEAR IS one of the major issues of our day. A study was conducted with five hundred people, asking them what their fears were in life. *Five hundred*, yet they listed over seven thousand fears!

John said, *"There is no fear in love. But perfect love drives out fear, because fear has to do with punishment. The one who fears is not made perfect in love"* (1 John 4:18). Those who are in fear today are those who do not seek the *Perfect Love* that drives away that fear. He replaces fear with joy and peace. Instead, they seek answers for their fear in the wisdom of the world. Jesus assured us that He indeed has *"overcome the world."*

The Choice Is Yours!

Fear! Fear! Such a terrible word!
Fear is the by-product of our modern world!

We seek all sources, our fear to rid!
We seek man's counsel for our souls to be fed!

Why do we want to live in fear,
when He who overcomes the world is so near?

When all is exhausted, and fear still endures,
will we seek the Source of Joy?
The choice is yours!

❧ THE PASTOR

IF A leader has never felt the pain of loneliness, then he or she probably has never really been a leader. Loneliness is inevitable in any leader's life! Leaders understand that they cannot always please everyone. Many times that opens the door to rejection and loneliness.

If that's you, then you're in good company, my friend. Take a look at these *leaders*, and then thank God He gave you the privilege to follow in their footsteps.

The Loneliness of Leadership

Noah decided God's will was a boat!
The people said in jest, *"It'll ne'er float!"*

Abram decided to share Canaan's feast!
Lot's bunch, perturbed, moved to the east!

David decided to slay the big giant!
Saul, in his pride, was certainly defiant!

Moses decided God's will was to roam!
The Israelites cried, *"Why don't we go home?!"*

Joshua decided Jericho could be won!
The majority rebuked, *"It can ne'er be done!"*

Elijah decided at Mt. Carmel to stand!
Israel's priests became *"toast"* on the land!

Paul decided that grace was the key!
Alexander, for control, stung him like a bee!

Peter decided to obey God's compelling!
The keepers of the Law called it rebelling!

Jesus decided the Father's will be done!
The people said, *"No!"* And with nails He was hung!

Leaders oft' are lonely when decisions are tough!
But, *"My grace,"* God said, *"is more than enough!"*

As a pastor, did you ever sit in your office, all alone and feeling like a failure? We get that way many times, I believe, because we lose sight of our own focus. In times like this, we only need to let God remind us first of why He led us into the ministry, and then why He led us to that particular church. I have had to do this more than once. This next poem was one of those times!

Why Did I Come?

Why did I come as a shepherd to you?
To ensure the Kingdom your budget did pursue?
Did I come to be there when the pain was intense?
Did I come to comfort when life made no sense?

Why did I come to this church so grand?
Did I come to cry with you and hold your hand?
Did I come to laugh when nothing seemed funny?
Did I come to kid with you and call you *honey*?

Why did I come when attendance was low?
Did I come with ideas to help you grow?
Did I come to a neighborhood at the end of its rope?
Did I come to replace their struggling with hope?

Why did I come when young families were obscure?
Did I come to ensure their children were secure?
Did I come with answers to meet their need?
Did I come with worship styles from which
they could feed?

Why did I come with so many to reach?
Did I come just to fill the duty to preach?
Did I come to make it quick, due to your hurry?
Did I come with a message in time to bury?

Why did I come? Only God knows the why!
Maybe to reassure eternal life when we die!
Maybe to teach Great Commandments from above!
That is, maybe to teach you simply . . . *how to love!*

THE FUNERAL

I'M SURE all of us as pastors have had that one special member within the Body; the person who was the picture of Kingdom service beyond all others. This was the case with "Shorty" Nash. I buried this wonderful man at the ripe old age of one hundred two! The man was an active deacon, sang in the choir, and even drove his own car until three months before he passed away.

What a remarkable Christian! He had seen it all, heard it all, and probably done it all, when it came to church. He was a blessed, wise and valuable resource from whom I sought counsel on many occasions. Let me introduce Mr. "Shorty" Nash. I wrote this poem upon the occasion of his very peaceful and quiet death.

Young pastors, listen to the wisdom of such men!

A Tribute to "Shorty" Nash

His name failed to match his many years here on earth;
long they were—one "O" two, from his birth!

Years filled with joy, filled with laughter, wit and grace;
the smile we always saw, seemed permanent on his face!

Snowy hair, softly flowing, gloriously crowning
suits so fine!
His quest—honor God with both appearance
and with mind!

A voice! What a voice! Songs echoed from his heart!
His role in the choir, one can ne'er fill his part!

Articulate, yet gentle, ever clear to the end;
O the wisdom he bestowed, how we long to hear again!

Only love, grace and faithfulness, his living lesson
was so good!
Clearly he defined what it means to "*walk with God!*"

HERE IS another great Christian man, whom I had the distinct pleasure of knowing. A small man in stature, yet a huge heart filled with compassion and commitment. The church received quite a shock when Mel suddenly died from a heart attack. They also soon learned that when he went to be with the Lord, this small man left an enormous hole to fill.

A Portrait of Mel

A quiet, gentle man was Mel,
on that we could all agree.
His love and mercy kept us warm,
truly Christ's masterpiece of harmony.

O church, the Godly wisdom of this man,
our souls it would surely feed.
His servant's heart of sacrifice,
ensured our every need.

Although his stature was shorter than most,
five foot six in all,
A spiritual giant was he in life,
in that he stood eight feet tall.

The image of Christ should be our aim,
in Mel that goal was clear.
And now he lives his favorite promise,
"we shall be like Him, when He appears!"
(1 John 3:2)

HOLLIS C. Roberts, my father-in-law, was one of the most gentle and loving men I have ever known. He rarely spoke, but when he did, his words were filled with purpose! I know he is the one who taught my wife to live with this phrase, "*Say what you mean and mean what you say!*" She often reminded me of that wise saying on many occasions throughout our marriage!

Hollis loved three things the most—his Lord, his family, and his garden. He was passionate for all three, and it showed in his everyday life. I wrote this poem, the week he passed away, as a tribute of love to him, wanting it to serve as a permanent reminder of what kind of man he truly was.

His Garden, His Passion
A Tribute to My Father-in-Law, Hollis C. Roberts

His garden, his passion, Hollis yearned for the Spring!
Alas! Time to plant, he and his birds did sing!
Slowly he tilled and prepared all the soil,
making rows proper depth, so the seed would not spoil.

Everyday to his passion he slowly did stroll,
to see if new sprouts had begun to unfold!
Soon they appeared, and with a smile on his face,
he silently thanked the Lord for His grace.

Weeding and hoeing, 'twas not work at all,
only pampering his passion 'til finally came Fall.
Potatoes, tomatoes, cucumbers, corn;
only a few of what filled his plentiful horn.

Much could be learned as he tended his passion,
one could clearly see the heart God had fashioned.
For deep within it God's love was secure,
and while growing a family he showed it for sure!

Everyday to his passion he strolled home tired and sore,
seeking the sprouts of joy he adored.
As he saw each one bearing supper, toads or lace,
he silently thanked the Lord for His grace.

Feeding and bestowing his love for them all,
he pampered his passion 'til winter's call.
When he quietly left garden, children and wife,
and met the Source of his passion—the Tree of Life!

THE PAIN

Now I want to share with you a personal work. My wife, Diane, was diagnosed with breast cancer in November, 2003. This came immediately after she had just recovered from her second neck vertebrae-fusion surgery. Her first words to me after the diagnosis was, *"The fun just never ends, does it?!"*

Unfortunately, we had just been called from our church in Jacksonville, Florida, to serve as pastor of a church in Knoxville, Tennessee. The timing could not have been any worse! She completed her radiation treatment by the end of December of that year, at which time I had to go to Tennessee and leave her in Florida. There were two reasons for this. First, she needed to stay with the oncologists who had been treating her, so they could better help her through the next four months of chemo-therapy. Second, we had promised to begin serving the church in Tennessee by the beginning of the year, so we both agreed I should go serve, while also looking for a house to buy. The separation was tough. The church in Tennessee, however (bless their souls), graciously allowed me to return to Florida every three weeks to spend the week with Diane whenever she had a chemo treatment. Those three week periods in between treatments, however, were very lonely—even lonelier for Diane, although my daughter was living with her at the time.

So, I wrote this poem just to her. A poem to show my love for her, and to assure her, as *one flesh*, I was hurting, too! Although meant to bring only her comfort in her time of need, God has opened many doors for me to share this poem with husbands whose wives were battling with breast cancer, or any other debilitating disease. Possibly, you can use the poem, too.

My Hero, My Love

Although the trial you now endure grows
weary and O so old;
keep trusting God *"who knows your way,
for after this test, you'll come forth as gold."*
(Job 23:8–10)

I know the suffering plagues your mind,
it seems strange, yea so unreal;
but God has said,
"Rejoice, my child, because His glory He will reveal."
(1 Peter 4:12–13)

Quietly you sit, no one around,
the anguish seems yours alone!
Untrue! I'm with you! My very being aches,
For *"one flesh we are, bone of my bones."*
(Genesis 2:23)

So fight on brave mate, my hero, my love,
together we'll fend off alarm;
Just *"place me like a seal over your heart,
like a seal on your arm."*
(Song of Songs 8:6)

THE HOPE

FOUR YEARS later, on September 16, 2007, Diane lost her courageous battle, and my beloved wife of thirty-four years went home to be with the Lord. She did so, however, in glorious fashion.

About four weeks earlier, when she knew she was in trouble, she awoke in her hospital room with a keen sense of peace about her. She calmly looked over to me and said, "*Good morning. You know what I saw last night? An angel!*"

Of course, I asked her if she had been dreaming, and she replied, "*No! I was wide awake, and saw him standing at the foot of the bed! He said nothing, yet gave me the sweetest look.*"

A few hours before she passed away, my daughter and I were in her room holding her hands. She labored with her breathing and could barely speak. Yet, somehow, she was able to turn to me and strongly proclaim, "*Trumpets! I hear trumpets! Don't you hear them?*" Five times she repeated this statement!

In both instances, Diane certainly gave living reality to those precious words, "*I will never leave you nor forsake you!*" Through it all she taught me a valuable lesson, which is reflected in this next poem.

The Most Important

I held her hand, as she struggled for dear life;
I thought of great moments I had spent with my wife.
Hundreds, maybe thousands, they were all in a swirl;
the special ones, however, began to unfurl.

Those romantic encounters sensually filling the air;
the soft kisses and embraces that removed every care.
Her holding my hand as we walked in the night;
on a bench, eating ice cream, watching sailboats in flight.

The excitement and fear as three children she gave birth;
yet the pain and the anguish bore riches of true worth.
The plays, the concerts, the games they would play,
we watched with great joy as we cherished each day.

Santorini sunsets, as we dined o'er the sea;
can't remember the meal, only her eyes watching me.
Viewing whales and otters from the coast of Carmel;
how her heart filled with bliss, it was easy to tell.

What was most important of all the precious times?
Of the moments in life, what towered in her mind?
Was it camping around a fire in crisp, night air?
Was it cruising the Caribbean, with time unaware?

Then in the darkness, her labored voice began to untangle,
as she whispered *"I hear trumpets, the trumpets of angels!"*
Five times she declared of that glorious sound,
as her Lord 'twas lifting her soul from earth's bound.

(continued)

Then I realized the most important in her fifty-four years,
as I held on and kissed her through all of my tears.
She taught me a lesson, when her soul finally left,
most important is God's greeting,
when you take your last breath.

❦

THE WORLD still mocks the Creator of all things. They still scoff at His virgin birth. They insist on doubting every word written or said about Him. They laugh at and insult anyone who has ever proclaimed His coming, whether the first time or the Second Coming.

He's coming! He's coming! Just as He fulfilled His first prophetic coming, He will surely fulfill the next! Preach it, brothers! Never stop! My prayer is that I will be caught up in the air, while I am right in the middle of a sermon about His coming!

When Are You Coming?

"When are you coming?" asked ancients of old.
 "Where is your promise of rescue from woe?"

"When are you coming?" Young Mary despaired.
 "Ow! Joseph, 'tis now! Check that inn over there!"

"When are you coming?" the shepherds did ponder.
 "Oh, my! You scared us! In a manger o'er yonder?"

"When are you coming?" the magi did query.
 *"Could that bright star o'er yonder
 lead to hope for the weary?"*

"When are you coming?" we asked so reposed.
 "The day nor the hour, no one really knows!"

"When are you coming?" the world mocks in fun.
 "No King today! Let's continue to run!"

"When am I coming?" thunders the Lord of Might.
 "Don't think of when, but as a thief in the night!"

"When are you coming?" the question still looms.
 "Just look around you! It has to be soon."

"I'm discouraged!"

"I'm so worried I don't know where to turn!"

"God's not listening to my prayers!"

"Everything seems hopeless now!"

"What can I do with my child? Where did I go wrong!"

E VER HEARD these words, Pastor? Many times, I'm sure! The world has never had the answer, yet, so many (including Christians) still seek its wisdom in time of need.

Jesus Christ is the only Hope! May we never preach or teach any other solution for despair!

Where Is the Hope?

"*Where is the hope?*" the Children of Israel complained!
 "*Too long in slavery we've had to reside!*"
Yet, God in His timing said with all His love,
 "*You're not only free, but take these
 Egyptian riches beside!*"

"*Where is the hope?*" Joe and Dan must have wondered.
 "*We're captive as slaves and defenseless!*"
Yet, God in His timing said with all His love,
 "*How'd you two like to be princes?*"

"*Where is the hope?*" Ol' Job certainly winced!
 "*I'm all alone, and these boils are not nice!*"
Yet, God in His timing said with all His love,
"*My purpose is complete, and to you my blessings twice!*"

"*Where is the hope?*" I hear some of you cry!
 "*This turmoil continues its looming!*"
Yet, God in His timing promised with all His love,
 "*My child, hang on, for I am coming!*"

THE GREATEST miracle of all—God raising Himself from the dead! We believe it happened through faith and the convincing power of His Holy Spirit. The world can't believe, because they have no faith and they have no Spirit.

How can we reveal such a saving miracle to a lost and dying generation? By living the life of the Risen Christ!

Live Again?

How can You cause a seed in the ground,
  although it is decayed in death;
  to raise in beauty the life of a rose,
  that simply takes away my breath?

How do You take the bulbs resting deep
  in the blackness of covered earth,
and burst them into rows of color-filled tulips,
  all dancing the song of new birth?

None of these miracles have yet been explained,
  though scientists accept them exact;
Yet the miracle of Christ, once dead but now alive,
  they still deny it's a fact.

Proving the case of the *empty tomb*,
  is not easy within the knowledge of men!
No, Your living Son is best revealed,
  by the new lives of the truly born again!

PAUL SAID, "For since the creation of the world God's invisible qualities—His eternal power and divine nature—have been clearly seen, being understood from what has been made, so that men are without excuse" (Rom 1:20).

If you ever (and you will) run into someone who doubts God's existence, or one of your members who is having a difficult time feeling God's presence, maybe this poem can help!

I Hear Your Song!

I *hear* Your song, Lord, in the morning I awake to its call.
The dove, mourning softly a reminder of my sin,
blends with the sparrow, sweetly singing
Your grace for all.
(1 Tim 13–14)

I *see* Your song, Lord, Your dynamics direct each phrase.
Rose petals and grazing deer call for piano,
while mountains crescendo Your majestic fortes!
(Psalm 8; Isaiah 55:12)

I *feel* Your song, Lord, its music touches my cheek as a kiss.
The softness of a breeze, the warmth of the sun,
the grass beneath my feet,
all convince me, Lord, You exist.
(Romans 1:20)

Your song, O Lord, a whisper of calm,
I *feel*, I *see*, I *hear*;
Though life's fire and wind and earthquakes roar,
You're not in them, You're near!
(1 Kings 19:11–12)

"*Your music is void in my life,*" you cry.
"*I've searched for it O so long!*"
Be still and know that He is God,
and quickly you'll sense His song!
(Psalm 46:10)

❧ The Commitment

I IMAGINE you've never had a member who has been too busy to serve!

Surely you've never had a member who's worried about the complexity of life!

Tell me you've never had a member who was enthralled with their own personal self esteem!

I'm certain you've never had a member that gave the *evil eye* to a guest entering the church with long hair, tattoos or possibly of different skin color!

Yeah, sure! We all have had to deal with them. Normally, these types of members have never really figured out the true purpose in life. Maybe this next poem can help them get their priorities straight.

Things God Won't Ask on that Day

God won't ask what kind of car you drove,
He'll ask how many people you drove
who didn't have transportation!

God won't ask the square footage of your house,
He'll ask how many people you welcomed into your home!

God won't ask about the clothes you had in your closet,
He'll ask how many needy you clothed!

God won't ask what your highest salary was,
He'll ask if you compromised your character to obtain it!

God won't ask what your job title was,
He'll ask if you performed your job to the best
of your ability!

God won't ask how many friends you had,
He'll ask how many people to whom you were a friend!

God won't ask in what neighborhood you lived,
He'll ask how you treated your neighbors!

God won't ask about the color of your skin,
He'll ask about the content of your character!
(Matthew 25:40)

*R*EVIVAL! THE church must have revival, if it is to be effective in today's New Age world!

Scripture tells us that Jesus began His ministry with this word, *"Repent!"* In fact, it says that He *"kept onsaying it"* the rest of His ministry here on earth. May these next two poems help you in getting this message across to your flock!

On Bended Knee

On bended knee, I pray with my heart!
I long for your presence, Lord!
Oh please ne'er depart!

On bended knee, I pray with my heart!
My sins, Lord, to Thee,
I humbly impart!

On bended knee, I pray with my heart!
Protect us I plead,
From Satan's deadly darts!

On bended knee, I pray with my heart!
To love all my brothers,
Reconcile if we part!

On bended knee, I pray with my heart!
That we do this together,
For revival to start!

A Revival Prayer

"Revive my church!" to the Lord I do plea!
"Seek My face," He replies, *"and repeat after me!"*

"Humbly I know I am nothing before Thee,
Your majesty and glory doest drive me to my knees!
The wickedness displayed through selfishness and pride,
I lay at your feet and turn it aside.

My Savior you are, indeed I admit,
but, Lord of my life, I've yet to submit!
My life is now yours to lead and direct;
e'en troubles and trials, Your glory may they effect.

Both faith and hope in You should I rest,
but without love from my heart, the two ne'er exist!
Created to serve in love, You have said;
thus, in love will I work, lest my faith is dead!

'Make disciples' the greatest commission for me;
my purpose in life! I dedicate it to Thee.
Show me my gifts, and the method to employ;
may Your Kingdom they build, as they spread Your joy!"

"If you pray this sincere, I will surely renew,
and my eyes, my ears, my heart will be in view!
When all of you do this, I want you to know,
My Spirit will heal, and your church will grow!"
(2 Chronicles 7:14–15)

❧ THE ADVENT

CHRISTMAS IS never a *"most wonderful time of the year"* for the many who are hungry, homeless, addicted to drugs and alcohol, or struggling with an unlimited list of battles that take the joy out of life.

Do you know someone like this? Does your church? One of my churches was surrounded by people like this in the community! In fact, we had fourteen Steps Houses/Halfway Houses within a five-block radius of the church.

What can you or your church do to possibly help those in misery to get a new start? What can be done to bring the joy of Christmas back into their lives again?

Where Did Christmas Go?

Where did Christmas go?
Family and laughter and spirits of good cheer;
why now the silence, all alone in my fear?

Where did Christmas go?
'Twas a time of hope, good will t'ward all men;
now, I wince at the thought of a new year again!

Where did Christmas go?
I see no tree, no tinsel, no twinkling lights;
only darkness of life and the battles I fight!

Where did Christmas go?
Once there were sugar plums dancing in my head;
now it is filled with nagging demons instead!

Where did Christmas go?
Can someone help me find it, please?
Is it still in the Child who came to set us free?

Where did Christmas go?
You say He's living in your heart?
I beg you, can you share Him,
and maybe give me a new start?

THERE IS another group of people who have a difficult time during the Christmas season. Many times, in all the excitement of Christmas musicals, children's plays, Christmas missions offerings, Christmas parties, Hanging of the Greens services, and a number of those normal things churches are supposed to do in December, we often forget about this group of people. People who were once the leaders in all the excitement! People who were once the supporters of the efforts! People who were all wrapped up in the glory of Christmas, just like us!

Now, these same people sit alone, either at home, or in a small room at the local nursing home. They are dreaming about Christmas past, and how much they would love to be involved again!

Do you have any members like this? What are you doing to make *sugar plums* dance in their heads one more time? What are you doing to restore their excitement for Christmas?

I Was Once There!

I was once there, 'midst the excitement of the year!
O, my little ones, how I loved to give you
Christmas cheer!

I was once there, wrapping gifts with love at night,
so to see your sleepy eyes begin to sparkle at first light.

I was once there, sitting at the Christmas table;
eating turkey, passing 'taters, downing goodies,
if we were able!

I was once there, with my family of the church;
O, how I loved to come, as we celebrated His birth!

I was once there, but no longer can I be;
for now I sit alone tonight, struggling with memories!

I was once there, but can you come now to me?
Maybe we can somehow make it the way it used to be!

M Y WIFE and I loved to entertain at Christmas. Diane went all out in preparing about twenty different kinds of Christmas *goodies* for all who came to our home and enjoyed.

We had such a gathering at our home when I was a pastor in Tennessee. It was our way of saying *"thank you"* for all the church had done the previous year!

If you can, I highly encourage you to do the same for your congregation. If so, then maybe you can adapt this poetic invitation I wrote.

An Invitation for You!

It was months before Christmas,
and all through our heads,
we were thinking of you
and how you'd be fed.

You've been so faithful,
with your time and your smile,
It'll be quite special,
to make it worth while.

Now the wreaths are all hung,
and the house will be alight,
For you are the special one,
on this festive night.

In thanks for your loving support,
please be our guest;
this is our gift to you,
and here's the request:

From two o'clock on the 18th,
'til five o'clock that same day,
take Washington Pike eastward,
and stop at (my address) on your way.

For at that locale,
in decorative bliss,
our home will be open,
with yummy goodies to ingest!

Diane and I, dressed in splendid
Christmas red,
will be waiting for you!
What more can be said?

A T CHRISTMAS time, I always ponder on what it must have been like around the manger scene that glorious night! Can you imagine the thoughts racing through Mary's mind as she looked down upon her God squirming in her arms? Can you imagine the excitement on the faces of those blessed parents, chosen by God to bring His Son into the world and to raise their own Creator? The following poem expresses my own imagination about that wonderful moment!

Good Morning, My Child!

Good morning, my child, for the very first time!
I can't believe You finally are here!
I'm sorry! Swaddling clothes were all I could find!
My, Your little face beams with cheer!

Last night was certainly a rough one, my dear!
Alas! All rooms in the inn were full!
But Your birth was definitely drawing near,
This stable had to do! Even though, it is so dull!

Look over here, that's Your daddy on earth!
Really handsome I think, and he protects us from danger!
His name is Joseph! A real carpenter of worth!
He'll build You a crib, not this ol' manger!

I still don't know why Your real Father chose me!
Your angel said I'd found favor with Him!
All I know is I'm happy as can be!
Imagine delivering, my own Deliverer from sin!

Oh! That reminds me! Let me tell You Your name!
Your angel I mentioned gave it to us!
It's the one You chose from where You came!
It means *Savior!* Remember? It's Jesus!

So sleep little Jesus, You need Your rest!
E'en though these animals crowd your bed!
I'll ensure that You grow to be Your best!
For one day You'll take the throne of David!

THE PATRIOT

M AY WE never forget those who put themselves in harm's way to protect our country; likewise, we must certainly never forget those who have bravely served in the past, especially those who gave the ultimate sacrifice.

I served for nearly three decades in the United States Navy. Many of you have possibly served your country, too. You know the sacrifice, the fears and the loneliness of soldiers, sailors and airmen. Always take the time with your congregation to lift up these brave men and women in prayer, and never forget. May this poem help you do that!

All Alone

All alone, bitter cold, soaking wet, in foxholes lay,
"Who's there? Friend or foe?
O God, may it be okay!"

All alone, only stars, amidst waves breaking o'er,
"How I miss her! O the smile!
Will she e'er see me at the door?"

All alone, flying high, puffs of smoke, flack so near,
"O Lord, see me shaking?
Can't you please remove my fear?"

Thundering booms, whistling rounds,
as their buddies breathe no more!
Do they know, can they feel,
that you're praying from distant shore?

Some survived. Some were maimed.
Some gave lives to answer freedom's call;
May we always thank our Father,
for the bravery of them all!

Ne'er forget, before you sleep in warm beds
safe at home,
to thank soldier, sailor, and airman,
who alone in harm's way doest roam.

❧ THE OBSERVANCE

ONE OF the biggest mistakes I have ever made in my ministry was when I decided not to preach a Mother's Day message for my congregation in Florida. I forget the subject of my message that day, but it was definitely not in honor of *mama*! I was never allowed to forget it!

Depending on your congregation, try to avoid that mistake, if at all possible! Maybe this poem will help you in your effort!

A Mother's Day Thought

Mama, who is this Jesus I'm learning about?
Does He really live in Heaven?
Do you have any doubts?

Grandma, who is this Jesus spoke of Sunday morn?
Can you tell me what it means,
to again somehow be born?

Mama, who is this Jesus they say took my place?
On a cross He did die,
for my sins, by His grace?

Grandma, who is this Jesus proclaimed to have risen?
Is it true what He said,
He can free us from a prison?

Mama, who is this Jesus, God's gift from above?
Can He live in my heart?
Can I feel His love?

Mama and Grandma, is Jesus in view?
Does He live in your hearts?
Can I see Him in you?
(2 Tim 1:5)

SINCE I had made the mistake of missing Mother's Day, believe me, I never forgot about good ol' dad! Never!

God clearly lays the responsibility on the *father* to ensure his family is focused on the glory of His Kingdom! Fathers are to be the example in teaching the truths found in Scripture. A father best sets that example to his children by revealing the relationship of Christ and His Church in the way he treats their mother!

Hey, Dad!

Hey, Dad! Can we play ball?
I need your advice since I'm still quite small!
When on the mound, and I muster up nerve,
how do I throw a ball that will curve?

Hey, Dad! Can we go to the lake?
I need your advice on what lures to take!
Or what should I do when my line runs out fast?
'Cause I have on the hook, a largemouth bass!

Hey, Dad! Can we go for a drive?
I need your advice to keep me alive!
At a four-way stop, who has right of way?
Ten o'clock and two, are my hands okay?

Hey, Dad! I think I have a date!
I need your advice to make it top rate!
Should flowers I bring, or candy in hand?
She's so pretty, she's so grand!

Hey, Dad! I'm engaged, believe it or not!
What should I do when I tie the knot?
Can I treat her like you did your beautiful bride?
Would mom agree that's the way I should abide?

Hey, Dad! You're a grandpa!, Your very first!
I'm so proud I'm about to burst!
How do I hold it? Do I feed when he cries?
Why do I melt when I look into his eyes?

(continued)

Hey, Dad! You've been great, my strength from birth!
Thank you for teaching God's love and its worth!
Can I take what you've taught, and share it with mine?
Can I e'er be like you, or will it take time?